Barbara Jean Barbara Jean Poetry

A Silhouette of Me

BJ Whittington

THOU Management, Inc.

c/o Publishing Dept

Barbara Jean Barbara Jean Poetry - A Silhouette of Me

THOU Management Inc.

c/o Publishing Dept

Post Office Box 913

Conley, Ga. 30288

ISBNs 13 978-0-9820080-1-0

Library of Congress Control Number: 2009932915

Library of Congress Subject Headings:

American poetry 21st century

African Americans -- Poetry

First Edition 2009

Cover Photography and book design by

THOU Management, Inc.

c/o Publishing Dept

www.thoupublishing.ning.com

1.0

This book is dedicated to my heirs, TJ & Tyhela Whittington. You are my life, my love, my legacy. My prayer is that you exceed my expectations with integrity and literally be transposed by exposing this scripture in your daily walk with Christ: but the people who know their God shall be strong, and carry out great exploits. Daniel 11:32b New King James

CONTENTS

Introduction

My inspiration for writing "***The Psyche of a Poet***" was...

I was reading a colleague's poetry book and I thought, "I have a sneak peak of who he is." This poem is dedicated to all the poets...

By reading this book
You get to see and look

A glance of who I am
A glimpse of what's in my brain

This is the risk of being a poet
Your secrets are unveiled for all to know it

Who you are a sneak peak of you
Revealing your thoughts through peek-a-boo

That's the beauty of this talent
Open the pages and I will let you in...

The Psyche of a Poet

I
Book
Of
Love

My inspiration for writing *"**The Love Chapter**"* was...

All these years I thought I had experienced love whereas I had rejected love – if I had at anytime rejected what's written in this poem or My Heavenly Father who is above. 1st Cor. 13:4–8 states "Love is patient, love is kind. It does not envy, it does not boast, it is not proud. It is not rude, it is not self-seeking, it is not easily angered, and it keeps no record of wrongs. Love does not delight in evil but rejoices with the truth. It always protects, always trusts, always hopes, and always perseveres. Love never fails..."

Love motives are unconditional
Love takes no regard of disposition

Love pierce through your spirit
And love all of you – your faults and issues

Love knows when to let go
When to say yes – when to say no

Love knows when you're carrying a heavy load
Love can discern a troubled soul

Love always wants the best for you
Love never holds back on the truth

Love gives unselfishly
Love treats one respectfully

Love gives no count to time
Love is gracious; love is kind

Love looks into your beautiful mind
And sees no evil – love is blind

Love needs no reason or no rhyme
To shower with gifts – to wine & dine

Love motto is "Whatever it takes"
Love companions with patience and say, "I'll wait"

Love play no games, tell no tales
Love is everlasting – love never fails

The Love Chapter

My inspiration for writing "***A Promise to Keep - A Recipe for Marriage***" was...

I was asked by my nephew to write a poem for his wedding. I had been waiting to be inspired and my inspiration arrived when all attendants were asked at his co-ed wedding shower to give advice to the soon to be newly wed couple. Asterisks & initials represent individuals' advice...

We are now joined together two as one heart
A promise to keep – till death do us part

From this day forward we will make all decisions together *WR*
A promise to keep, to love, obey and cherish

We will work together building a strong foundation **RJ*
And promise to keep open the lines of communication

I promise to love the good, the bad and the ugly**DL*
To stay together - A promise to keep from now and forever

We promise not to let the sun go down on our anger
I promise to you – My love I surrender

We promise to understand each other's fault**RJ*
And not to misinterpret your words for my thoughts

I promise to let no one get between you and me**DD*
We promise to keep our business discreet**MS*

We promise to pray constantly – without cease**EJ*
Remembering marriage takes three – God, you & me**RH*

We promise to seek God first in all that we do**TJ*
And let His plans unfold for me and you

We promise to study God's recipe for marriage
1st Corinthians 13 – The Love Chapter**VR*

And when times get hard we'll remember what a wise woman said
Marriage will only be successful when both parties make God their Head**BW*

A Promise to Keep
A Recipe for Marriage

My inspiration for writing "***A Revelation***" was...

I was hanging out with a male friend and we were getting a little bit too close. If you don't watch yourself and be conscious of your surrounding, love can sneak upon you. I always wondered about love; wanted to write about love; when do you know you are in love? ...

What is this thing called Love – is it really true
Or is it an infatuation to inspire fools

Can this thing love be easily pursued?
Do you have a choice or does love choose

Is it a game some play creating their own rules?
Do they not know that a player has to loose

Can it be an emotional high that puts you in a certain mood?
When you hear the lyrics to your favorite song – jazz, rock or blues

Some say it's an alibi for sex to comfort and soothe
Is this the truth – or is it a sorrowful excuse

Others call it false hope, chemistry, an essential nourishment – soul food
This thing we call love often is abused

Could it be a deceptive belief of one's perception – a delusion?
Or a mistaken visual misconception – an illusion

They say you can't hide when love is calling you
Why do they say --- I'm *falling* in love with you

A Revelation

My inspiration for writing "***A Silent Wish***" was...

Have you ever had a crush on someone and they did not know it? Well here it is in poetry... Oh, I know what you're thinking. Well Barbara did it ever happen? Some things should be kept silent. This is a wish for two hearts to kiss...

Glancing into your eyes makes my very essence melt

Wishing to share the sensations my heart has felt

Wondering what kind of hand is this I have been dealt

How did I get here is the question asked

Why do I feel so peaceful with you; so relaxed?

Have our souls been knitted together, connected, attached

It seems impossible, illogical, so unfair

I desire to hold you, kiss you, caress you – Do I dare?

I then whisper to destiny – only God's will is my prayer

A Silent Wish

My inspiration for writing ***Destiny***" was...

Sometimes when you see brothahs checking out sistahs you can interpret what they are saying by the expressions on their faces. Here's my translation...

When I first saw you – You were fine
I wondered to myself – What's on your mind
I rushed to meet you – Didn't want to waste time
And when you looked at me – I knew you were mine

Couldn't wait to find out what made you click
To talk with you and get your digits
I'm normally cool – but I felt a little fidget
My game was weak – Whereas I'm use to being rigid

But when you smiled – You made it worth my while
The way you stride – I knew you were my style
I wanted to ask – Would you be my wife?
What are you doing for the rest of your life?

And then I said – Take it slow
Don't be afraid – Time will show
The conversation in her head – So let it flow
The days will unveil – what Destiny already know

Destiny

My inspiration for writing "***LoveMaking***" was...

I was talking to someone and they told me he loved me. Immediately I knew he didn't and we had not yet scratched the surface of what love is - as we had experienced it. I then wondered can we "humans" truly love as God loves??!!...

Only God truly knows how to love
We are only imitators
At times perpetrating
Disguised, falsifying admiration – playing infatuation
Thinking we're LoveMaking
Hoping love won't find out we're faking

Yielding to our passions – placating
Pacifying sexual desire – allaying destination
Alleviating emotions to tranquilize pain – mitigating duration
Never giving – always taking
This is what we think – LoveMaking
Allow me to interrupt your imagination with an invasion of a revelation

Love isn't easily figure out it's an ancient of days complication
Difficult to understand – an intricate situation
Often blowing your mind – excitingly breathtaking
Compassionately merciful with undeserving favor
Endlessly anticipating our arrival of faith
Persistently preserving life - saving grace

Patiently awaiting the reality of fate
Never-ending, nevertheless never failing
Always prevailing
Collaborating with sympathy tolerating our errors and mistakes
Now let me reiterate what it takes
What Jesus did on the cross –

Now that's LoveMaking

LoveMaking

My inspiration for writing "**I Am Beautiful; I am Love 'N' Love loves Me**" was...

To speak a positive personal statement of words over myself, to myself so that it may reflect within myself and show without...

I am surrounded by love's passion
Saturated in love's perfection
Comforted in love's protection

I am beautiful; I am Love 'N' Love loves me

I am embraced by love's warm attachment
Captivated in love's charmed enchantment
Secured in love's arms of contentment

I am beautiful; I am Love 'N' Love loves me

I am magnetized by love's attraction
Mesmerized by love's attention
Motivated by love's affection

I am beautiful; I am Love 'N' Love loves me

I am absorbed in love's inspiration
Stimulated in love's exhilaration
Influenced by love's intoxication

I am beautiful; I am Love 'N' Love loves me

I am head over heels in love-struck
Smitten by love love-bug
Fallen in the sea of love

I am beautiful; I am Love 'N' Love loves me

I Am Beautiful; I am Love 'N' Love loves Me

II
Book
Of
Prayers
&
Worship

My inspiration for writing *"**A Prayer of Faith to Heal the Sick**"* was...

One day around Christmas 2008 my daughter got ill and I had to rush her to the emergency room. I was so scarred. That day is now considered one of the most traumatic days of my life. I knew the Word of God was powerful so I researched healing in the bible to gain strength and increase my faith. I was in the process of writing this poetry book and this is how the topic manifested itself in poetry...

O' hear our cry and take heed to our sighs
Jehovah-Raphah, Healer Our God
Incline thine ear and hear us now
Manifest Your glory right before our eyes
As we profess Your praises out loud

For Your people humbly call and pray
Turn to You seeking Your face
We ask that You forgive our sins
Restore health and heal our land
This we pray in Jesus' Name

Have compassion on us for we are weak
Heal us O Lord for our body is in agony
For Your touch we desperately need
For Thine is the Healer of all infirmities
And for this cause we bow our knees

For You were wounded for our transgressions
Took the whipping for our chastisements
Stood in the place for our punishments
Received the bruises for our iniquities
And by Your stripes we are healed

We stand on Your Word and do believe
Whom the Son set free is free indeed
Having faith the size of a mustard seed
Making our supplications known unto Thee
We take authority over this disease

We are the anointed with holy oil
And do all in the Name of the Lord
The prayer of faith will save the sick from turmoil
In the Name of Jesus the Christ they will rise and walk
For the effectual prayer of the righteous availeth much

Declaring and decreeing this is the time to heal
For God has not given us the spirit of fear
I AM – God - Our Healer is near
And Your healing power has appeared
For the kingdom of God has arrived here
AMEN

A Prayer of Faith to Heal the Sick

My inspiration for writing "***A Prayer for my Descendants***" was ...

When my children were in my womb I always prayed and desired that they have a personal relationship with God. One of my prayers was that they seek Him on their own early in childhood to obtain the greatest and best life possible. I continuously tell them that they must teach their children about God and His Word. And in order for that to come to past they must know God for themselves. So my mission was to train up my children in the way they should go; and that they and their descendants never depart from that training...

I pray today for my descendants
That You O Lord will be their inheritance
And their ear shall be Your attendance
Your will only shall be their allegiance

For my children is the kingdom of God
This I pray and declare out loud
In faith I believe and do not doubt
Therefore my seed shall not be without

I declare this day that my child is safe
And their life is covered by Your amazing grace
That Your heavenly angels protect them everyday
In all their days they seek Your face

I thank You Father that my children come to You
Asking the question what shall I do
That You are with them to see them through
To follow the plans that You had drew

I thank You Lord that You have taken them in Your arms
Secured and protected them from all harm
Laid hands on them and touched their heart
Broken, blessed and set them apart

To do the will of the kingdom of God
Manifesting the fruit of the Spirit from heaven above
For my children are an inheritance from the Lord
The fruit of my womb – an exceeding great reward
AMEN

A Prayer for My Descendants

My inspiration for writing "***A Prayer for Wisdom***" was ...

I always wanted to obtain godly wisdom and I believe that others desire it too. So I researched it. The following verses expound upon this treasure: Ps. 111: 10 states the fear of the Lord is the beginning of wisdom; Pro. 8: 11 states that wisdom is better than rubies; Prov. 16:16 states that wisdom is better than gold; Eccles. 9:16 states wisdom is better than strength; and Eccles. 9:18 states wisdom is better than weapons of war. I believe that wisdom is an attribute of God that every child should hunger for...

Father this day I pray for wisdom
Seeking first Thy kingdom come
In reverence and fear Thy will be done
For truly this is wisdom's foundation

Make me wise and give me understanding
So that I may have abundance of life everlasting
For You desire honesty from the heart
Help me to be truthful in my inner thought

What You are after is truth from the inside
Please enter me that I may conceive new life
Make me righteous and fill my judgment with insight
Enlarge my territory and let there be light

Teach me Lord to make wise of my time
For Your commandments is my constant guide
Touch my mouth and put wisdom in my mind
So that I may discern right and grow wise

Show me Lord wisdom's innermost secrets
And hide Your face from mine iniquities
Make me wiser that my enemies
For I always consider Your decrees

Let not my response be with empty knowledge
Make me to understand Thy loving kindness
Grant me keen instinct and powerful intuition
Cause Your wisdom to come into fruition

Humble me and give me godly revelation
For Your Word is my daily meditation
Let kindness rule when I give instruction out
And wisdom be my source when I open my mouth
AMEN

My inspiration for writing "***December 20, 2007***" was...

It was five days prior to Christmas and every year I would get depressed around the holidays. Then I made a conscious decision that I would not have anymore bad Christmases. This poem was written because I had to encourage myself and speak to my situation; and remind me, who masters me...

As I'm absorbed in my misery
The eyes of my understanding enlighten me
A revelation finally hit me
And God's wisdom starts to speak to me
So I declare to my disparity
And I say to my enemy
What I know You are to be
You Are God!

I remind my poverty
Who You are economically
Jehovah-Jireh my providence source of eternity
I reiterate to the innermost part of me
Who is the creator of my anatomy
Be still and know I AM sent me
And greater is He within me
You Are God!

To the fear within me
That constantly tries to taunt me
The Lord is here who said, "Let there be"
And light appeared that all might see
You are the standard in Excellency
My banner for all to see
Jehovah – Nissi that's who You be
You Are God!
I recite to the darkness that tries to surround me
And speak to the chains that attempt to hold me
Loose me and set me free
I am far above all principalities
I no longer live in captivity
And nothing is able to contain me
Not even earth's gravity
Because......**You Are God!**

December 20, 2007

My inspiration for writing "***A Psalm of Barbara***" was...

There are times when it seems that the enemy has turned up the heat on you. You can sense and discern that he is trying to plot against you. This is the time when you need to go into prayer. Psalms are considered an assortment of prayers, poems and hymns that are sacred. This is a prayer that was written because I had a rough day at work...

Cast me not away from Thy presence
Into my heart please take residence
Let not mine enemy violate my existence

Ground my feet – root it in perseverance
Til the core of my essence glory in Your reverence
Does not Your Word endure forever?

Til it's fulfilled to every letter
Causing all things to work together
Exposing the thoughts of the enemy's endeavors

As it is written in the scriptures
You reveal Your secrets to Your servants
That Your knowledge may be relevant

Making man's eyes wonder in awe
And the seed of Abraham glory in their God
Rejoicing in the love You have for us

So stretch forth Your mighty hand
And expose the secret Master plan
That the earth is the Lord's and does not belong to man
SELAH

A Psalm of Barbara

My inspiration for writing, "***Don't Let Me Leave You***" was...

I was reminded of the scripture that said, "God would never leave us or forsake us" and I thought, "He won't but we have." I then prayed this prayer...

Don’t ever let me leave You -
Always remind me that You are near
Give me an eye to see – an ear to hear

A word, a warning or a sign
That You are with me every time

If I don’t know that You are with me
I won’t know that I’m pleasing Thee

I need to know that I have Your blessing
I need to know what You’re thinking

I realize You won’t leave me nor forsake me -
What I’m concerned about is me leaving You

The path I’m taking, my dreams, my pursuit –
Am I blinded by my own truth –
Are my decisions lined up with You?

This is why I need a sign
A warning, a witness, a Word from on high

To let me know I have not gone astray
And squandered my inheritance in my own way

So I seek You with all my heart
To know your plans; to know your thoughts

And I pray...

Don’t ever let me leave You -
Always remind me that You are near
Give me an eye to see – an ear to hear

Don’t Let Me Leave You

My inspiration for writing "***When Men Pray***" was...

One day I was pondering on some past experiences that I thought there was no logical answer. I said to myself there are some things in which we will never have answers. And then my thoughts stumbled upon a past relationship in which I thought was a divine appointment from God. I immediately had doubts about the encounter until I was reminded by a still soft voice. "It's not that God did not answer, we often ask God for something and when it comes we don't want it at the time; or we wanted it in a certain way, form or fashion; or we didn't expect it to come." But He does answer when we pray...

When men pray God answers
It might manifest immediately, rapidly or be delayed
You may be a coward, bold, shy or afraid
God responds to every bowed head

When men pray God answers
It may appear hazy, far away or even foggy
You might be blind, sightless with a splinter in your eye
But God hears every child's cry

When men pray God answers
It may not come now, today or even tomorrow
As long as you bow and reverence Thou Name is hallow
God adheres to every sorrow

When men pray God answers
It might not be the way you envisioned it to see
A specific length, figure, shape or size
God is attentive to our every cry

When men pray God answers
The response might be instant, soon or long
Your plea may be silent, verbal or a groan
But God listens to our every moan

When men pray God answers
It might be for a friend, neighbor, son or daughter
Your words might be lengthy, few, longer or shorter
God received your request once you brought it to the altar

When men pray God answers
It might seem like more than you can bear
You might go to Him daily, often or rare
God accepts every vessel's prayer

When men pray God answers
Men should never cease to pray
Always seek God to make a way
Have you fallen on your knees today?

When Men Pray

My inspiration for writing ***"Your Word"*** was...

I was studying the bible and realized how powerful the Word of God is...

In Your Word is my liberty
My pardon and release from captivity
Your Word and commandments have set me free
From the power of the hands of my enemy

Words of history that had taunt me
Words from others that were spoken over me
Words of yesterday that lingered generationally
Words of my past that echoed continuously

Your Word became flesh and dwelt among men
Your Word came to save not to condemn
Your Word came and destroyed sin
Your Word is eternal and shall never end

Thank You for Your Word which the Sprit was conceived
That the Word gave life into us it breathe
The Spirit of adoption we have received
All because of Your Word we have believed

Your Word

My inspiration for writing '***Psalm 151***" was...

This poem was written as ministry to the Lord by way of poetry. When we minister to others we are ministering to the God within them. When you help others you are helping God. This is the epitome of the scripture in Matthew 25: 35-40 which states: For I was hungry and you gave me something to eat, I was thirsty and you gave me something to drink, I was a stranger and you invited me in, I needed clothes and you clothed me, I was sick and you looked after me, I was in prison and you came to visit me. "Then the righteous will answer him, 'Lord, when did we see you hungry and feed you, or thirsty and give you something to drink? When did we see you a stranger and invite you in, or needing clothes and clothe you? When did we see you sick or in prison and go to visit you? "The King will reply, 'I tell you the truth, whatever you did for one of the least of these brothers of mine, you did for me.' It has its title because there are 150 psalms in the bible. This is Psalm 151...

I desire to worship Thee
In You only is my liberty
On one accord in perfect peace

Awaiting Your arrival is where You'll find me
In Your presence is where I long to be
In the beauty of holiness forever with Thee

Alone with My covering – lost in serenity
Basking in Your love – Your glory surrounding me
Words can't explain – Holy hovering over me

Whisper who I am – bring it to my memory
Thou art My refuge, My hiding place – My security
Where I can vanish in obscurity – a place to retreat safely

This is where I yearn to be – in the presence of Royalty
With My Lord, My Love – King of Eternity
My Hope, My Peace, My Grace & Mercy

Psalm 151

My inspiration for writing "***Holy Ground***" was...

This poem is a song from my heart based on Ex. 3:5 "Do not come any closer," God said. "Take off your sandals, for the place where you are standing is holy ground..."

Remove your sandals from your feet
For the place where you stand is Holy Land
Where God will meet you at the mercy seat
Lift up your hands and praise His Name
Surrender your heart and bow your knees
Joining with the seraphims - Holy, Holy, Holy

Praising His Name and singing out loud
I'm Walking with God on Holy Ground

For where we stand is Holy Land
A place to retreat – God inside of me
I AM WHO I AM is forever your name
Seated with Christ in the heavenly
We minister to You in worship today
We touch and agree Your will we pray

Praising His Name and singing out loud
I'm Walking with God on Holy Ground

We turn aside and see this great sight
Angels rejoicing all around
Praising You Lord with all of our might
On Holy Ground where Your face can be found
We surrender all and give You our life
I am interruption in my bloodline

Praising His Name and singing out loud
I'm walking with God on Holy Ground

Here we bow at the mountain of God
Amazing grace - I can see the light
Singing to God a new sound
For Your Spirit to lead and guide
Praying Your kingdom to come now

Praising His Name and singing out loud
I'm walking with God on Holy Ground

Holy Ground

My inspiration for writing ***"You Are My God – How Great Thou Are"*** was...

One day, while at work I had this overwhelming emotion in my spirit that I could not explain or was I able to interpret. The only words I can find in my vocabulary to describe this feeling was peculiar, weird, odd; and I didn't know if the feeling was good or bad. It's been said that God's glory is weighty, heavy.

So I went to the church grounds and prayed.
After worshipping this is what my spirit said;
This is what I was fed;
These are the lyrics I heard in my head...

You are my God
You are my peace in the midst of the storm
How great Thou are
We enter in
And with the angels cry Holy

Your are my God
You are my shelter in You I am at home
How great thou are
We enter in
Into the chambers of Your Majesty

You are my God
You are My Refuge – I am safe from all harm
How great Thou are
We enter in
Into the presence of Your glory

You are my God
You are my help - can't face these trials all alone
How great Thou are
We enter in
Into the grace of the mercy seat

You are my God
You are My Hope – this is why I can go on
How great Thou are
We enter in
Where the Spirit of the Lord is – Our Liberty

You are my God
You are my joy – I can sing all day long
How great thou are
I've entered in
Into the life Christ died for me
His blood has set me free
And I got the victory
I give all praises to Thee!

You are my God
How Great Thou Are

My inspiration for writing "***The Gift of the Holy Spirit***" was...

I wanted to thank God for the gift of the Holy Spirit, which is God literally living inside of us. The Holy Spirit is a precious deposit in our bodies, the temple of God. Luke 11:13 states if you then, though you are evil, know how to give good gifts to your children, how much more will your Father in heaven give the Holy Spirit to those who ask him. SELAH...

We thank You that we have received the gift of the Holy Spirit
We are baptized with fire in the Holy Spirit
We are filled with the promised Holy Spirit

We are blessed and led by the Holy Spirit
We are full of joy in the Holy Spirit
We receive power from the Holy Spirit

You breathed on us and we have received the Holy Spirit
It is not us speaking, but the Holy Spirit
We speak in other tongues enabled by the Holy Spirit

We receive from the Father the promised Holy Spirit
We are full of faith in the Holy Spirit
We are encouraged by the Holy Spirit

We believed to receive the Holy Spirit
We are warned by the Holy Spirit
Your Love is poured into our hearts by the Holy Spirit

Our conscience is confirmed in the Holy Spirit
We overflow with hope by the power of the Holy Spirit
We are sanctified by the Holy Spirit

Our body is the temple of the Holy Spirit
We have received the fellowship of the Holy Spirit
We are sealed with the promised Holy Spirit

We have the fruit of the Holy Spirit
We do not grieve the Holy Spirit
We guard the good deposit with the help of the Holy Spirit

We have tasted the heavenly gift shared in the Holy Spirit
We enter into the Most Holy Place by the Holy Spirit
We receive testimony from the Holy Spirit

We are guided by the Spirit of Truth, the Holy Spirit
We have another Helper, the Holy Spirit
We are the work of the Holy Spirit

We build ourselves up in holy faith and pray in the Holy Spirit
We are saved through the washing of rebirth and renewal by the Holy Spirit
We have the grace of Christ, the love of God and the communion of the Holy Sprit

The Gift of the Holy Spirit

III
Book
Of
Exhortation
&
Literary Poetry

My inspiration for writing "***A Wealthy Place***" was...

Simply put I was tired of not having enough money to support my family and me. So I started speaking to the situation. Poverty is a place and as soon as we move (i.e. repent – change our mind). We will walk out of that cycle...

Because poverty is a state of mind
A wealthy place is where I reside

I refuse to empower impoverishment
And allow my intellect to lie dormant

To sit and embrace the comfort of stagnate
And steer my mental will incapacitate

I disallow the subtlety of destitute
Creeping in my head disguising the truth

Patiently expecting my dreams to come true
All the while my dreams awaiting me to produce

I resent the past that tries to keep me bound
By the pain my past left behind

The years that were stolen in a moment of time
While destiny processed my suspended mind

And caused my conscious to awaken and rise
Allowing revelation to ignite its shine

Bursting illumination through mine eyes
Rising above the currency of waves and tides

Because prosperity is now my state of mind
A wealthy place is where I will always abide

A Wealthy Place

My inspiration for writing "***A Visitation Expecting a Holy Habitation***" was...

I went to visit a friend and I was unable to see him. I became frustrated and dismayed because I thought that God sent me and the journey wasn't victorious – so I believed. And then God told me to get my mind off of me, pick up my pen and start writing. This is how He felt and it wasn't about me...

You called **Me** and **I** did come
Desiring for you and **I** to become one

Expecting not only a visitation
But an invitation for a holy habitation

You were unable to see **Me**
Because **I** was not your priority

You did not expect **Me** to come
Where are you getting this doubt from

Why do you fear - Ye of little faith
Why have you worry and cast **Me** away

I desire your eyes to behold **Me**
That you are released and set free

I am disappointed because you did not believe
I was hurt and My Spirit was grieved

But **I** kept My Word when **I** said
I will answer whenever you prayed

I haven't left nor forsaken you
You have strayed and miss-taken the truth

Give up your will and to **Me** surrender
Clear My Name so that **I** may enter

A Visitation Expecting A Holy Habitation

My inspiration for writing "***The Enemy Cannot Win – Ephesians 6:10***" was...

This poem was written because so often we look outside ourselves for the enemy and often the enemy is within. In order to combat the enemy you must rightly use the Word of God as Christ did. This poem is based on Ephesians 6:10 – 18. Finally, be strong in the Lord and in his mighty power. Put on the full armor of God so that you can take your stand against the devil's schemes. For our struggle is not against flesh and blood, but against the rulers, against the authorities, against the powers of this dark world and against the spiritual forces of evil in the heavenly realms. Therefore put on the full armor of God, so that when the day of evil comes, you may be able to stand your ground, and after you have done everything, to stand. Stand firm then, with the belt of truth buckled around your waist, with the breastplate of righteousness in place, and with your feet fitted with the readiness that comes from the gospel of peace. In addition to all this, take up the shield of faith, with which you can extinguish all the flaming arrows of the evil one. Take the helmet of salvation and the sword of the Spirit, which is the word of God. And pray in the Spirit on all occasions with all kinds of prayers and requests. With this in mind, be alert and always keep on praying for all the saints.

Searching outward looking around
For my enemy cannot be found

Where are you I know you're near
Trying to implant the spirit of fear

False evidence appearing real
Coming as a thief trying to steal

Always having the same routine
Your next attack is to kill our dream

Father of lies, deceit and fraud
Your final plan is then to destroy

But I have a message for you from above
You will not make the Word of God void

I will study to show myself approval of
By embracing God's letters of love

And rightly dividing the Word of truth
Like drawing near to God and He will draw near to you

And putting on the whole armor of God
Knowing every good gift comes from above

That faith without works is dead
And this is the day the Lord has made

Because greater is He within me
Resist the devil and he will flee

Renewing our mind to have the mind of Christ
For whoever believes in Him has eternal life

And finally my brethren, always fulfilling the first
commandment
By loving the Lord with all our heart, soul, mind and strength

The Enemy Cannot Win – Ephesians 6:10

My inspiration for writing "***The Process***" was...

This epic depicts waiting on God while you are going through trials and tribulations – The characteristics of a process...

During the process keep the faith
By trusting God while He's teaching you to wait
Knowing the testing of your faith produces patience
For The Lord your God is performing a major surgery
So let patience have its perfect way

Continue to read, study, fast and pray
Rejoice in the Lord and He will make a way
Jehovah-Jireh will provide your daily bread
But in order to please Him you must have faith
So your prayers won't be hindered or delayed

Lean not to your own understanding
By thinking, reasoning and second guessing
For His Holy Spirit will give you the answers
Then you will soar above your circumstances
And have peace that surpasses all understanding

Remember this stage is only temporary
A means to an end for your destiny
A tool, an instrument, a way, a route
This is only a path not your final stop
For the Lord your God will surely bring you out

Commit your way to Him and He will bring it to pass
And of all His good works you will declare
I will rejoice in the Lord for He has made me glad
Dwell in His name and He will not put you to shame
For it's better to trust in the Lord and not in man

Relax don't worry it's an open Book test
Trust in the Lord and you will find rest
Have faith in God and He will fulfill your request
Our God is Omnipotent – A Father that knows best
Don't give up, don't give in; don't despise the process

My inspiration for writing "***He has Caused All Things to Work Together***" was...

This poem is based on one of my favorite scriptures in the Bible – Romans 8:28 And we know that in all things God works for the good of those who love him, who have been called according to his purpose...

All things work together
Sunshine, rainy days – any kind of weather
The good, the bad, the ugly – the whatever
This too shall past and it's going to get better

For the good of those who love God
Pursuing Him with all their heart
Knowing He hears every time you call
And His presence is wherever you are

You are the called according to His purpose
The chosen to fulfill through prayer & worship
The elect He designed to display His splendor
To whom His will on one accord has surrendered

So it doesn't matter where you find yourself
Even if you can't find yourself
Rather if you are all by yourself
God is God all by Himself

And He has already gone before you begun
Numbered your days before you were born
Planned your destiny before you were formed
Answered your prayers before your were done

Caused your dry bones to live and flourish
Even though your plans were faulty and malnourished
You cry & pray "If I would've, could've, maybe, should"
In the end you will say, "He has caused all things to work out for my good"

He Has Caused All Things To Work Together

My inspiration for writing "***The Great Commission – Teachers to the Nations***" was...

I had taken a class at church and had to perform a demonstration of what I had been taught. So I wrote a song and had two students rap it for me. The Great Commission is our petition...

Jesus appeared to the eleven at the table
To make disciples of all populations
And preach the gospel to all creation
The Great Commission for Teachers to the Nations

He appeared and breathed peace be unto you
We suddenly received the Spirit of Truth
As the Farther has sent Me, so I also send you
He cast out doubt and some He rebuked

You believe because you have seen
Blessed are those who hasn't and still believe
These things were done that the scripture be fulfilled
They should look on Him whom they have pierced

Go into the entire world and preach
The kingdom of God to everyone you meet
He who believes and is baptized
Shall be saved and have eternal life

They will cast out demons in My Name
And will take up serpents into their hands
They will speak with new tongues
And not be hurt if they drink poison

As He appeared this was His speech
All authority has been given to Me
He gave the disciples His great charge
To baptize all near and far

In the name of the Father, Son and Holy Spirit
Teaching to observe all decrees He had given
All of the commandments to God and men
Including the Lord's Supper in this Great Commission

I am with you always until to the end of the age
In all circumstances I will supply you My grace
And with all that succeed you in future generations
This is The Great Commission for Teachers to the Nations
SELAH

The Great Commission – Teachers to the Nations

My inspiration for writing "***Sweet Words***" was...

I met a gentleman and he kept staring at me. His words were speaking volumes to my head. And as I was trying to sleep that night these ***Words*** just kept coming to me..........

Your words are the words that soothe me
Sounds of waves of words flow right through me
Swept away by your words – I'm loosing me
Got my mind playing tricks – go hide and seek
Lost in your words by your word – can you find me?
Mesmerized by your words in your words – what you saying to me
But I won't let the word of your words play on me

The way your words – say your words, enchant me
I'm like a donor in the hands of a philanthropy
Got me thinking in your words – they're drowning me
I'm sinking in your words – come swim with me
Like your word I like your words – come taste and see
Your words are so sweet – taste like honey bee
Playing words on your words – honey come see about me
But I won't let the word of your words capture me

Hear the word of your voice is what I need
I want your words – hear your words, here with me
To hear the touch of your words are you feeling me
The words of your sound how can this be
I'm sick needing your words – hear your words healing me
Say the word I need a word to hear a word set me free
All because your words are the words that captivated me

My inspiration for writing "***A Metamorphosis***" was ...

There comes a time when your life changes, you don't realize it has taken place and you've never experienced this before. There is no point of reference. You're going day by day and a transformation has approached. You get disgruntled, confused and you don't understand what's going on. One might say that change is good for you. But there are times when you are unaware that change has arrived without you inviting it...

He's in the recess of mind like a subliminal message yet unread
He's compressed in a moment of time in the corner of my head

Awaiting for his arrival – the fruition of the day
When the clock strikes twelve and time has made a way

Into my world of loneliness - fulfilling destiny
Changing my plan – altering my journey

Causing the season to spring forth
The wind to blow another course

The road less traveled – an unusual place
Broadening my horizon – invading my space

Challenging my schools of thoughts – my point of view
Compelling me to stop and think it through

Where did you come from – what is this?
A change in life – A Metamorphosis

A Metamorphosis

My inspiration for writing "***I Was Forsaken This One Thing***" is...

I wanted to write a poem where as my descendants would be studying poetic literature and the teacher decided to use this poem. The teacher will then say, "We have a student in this class that is related to the author." That would make my relative feel ten feet tall. The future has put a demand on this piece of poetry! This poem was written so that it can be dissected in literary classes all around the world...

I was forsaken this one thing
And midnight became my best friend
Shadows followed and I welcomed them in
Showers brushed the seasonal end

Was I forsaken this one thing

Now I know no other way
This thing comforts while I seize my prey
This thing confronts – watch my image decay
The colors of the rainbow fade away

Was I forsaken this one thing

Erasing the sketches from my canvas
Causing my ship to sail haphazard
Is the direction of the boot southward
A resting place for this thing burial

Was I forsaken this one thing

Is the clay, the mud, this thing; the remains
Left an embroidery in the depth of my brain
A piece of rag; a dirty stain
Blood from an animal cannot attain

Was I forsaken this one thing

The buzzing bee, an insect sting
An allergic reaction beneath the skin
Discharge pollen from a seed implant
Was I forsaken this one thing

Til destiny provoked this thing to end
I Was Forsaken This One Thing

My inspiration for writing "***I Love The Gift Inside of You***" was...

Everyone has been given gift(s) and it's a beautiful thing to see peoples' gift(s) on display. This poem is dedicated to my son and daughter...

I love the gift inside of you
The way you sing the words you say
The way you think – it blows my mind away

I love the gift inside of you
The way you are a superstar
You're going far as an actor

Boy, I love the gift inside of you
When I'm sad you make me laugh
You're very smart with the sweetest heart

I love the gift inside of you
The way you dribble that basketball
Cross them over and make them fall

Girl, I love the gift inside of you
You're extremely studious and very intelligent
You make them grades that stand for excellent

I love the gift inside of you
When it's dark or I'm feeling blue
You brighten my day when you do what you do

I love the gift inside of you
Reveal it, give it – let it be see through
Unwrap the gift so we can see what you do

I Love the Gift Inside of You

IV
Book
Of
Sisters

My inspiration for writing "***I Am Woman***" is...

To often we as women downgrade men with our mouth not realizing how powerful our words are. The bible states that death and life is in the power of the tongue (Pro. 18:21). And we as females were born as helpers which are the same characteristics defined as another Helper in the Bible, the Holy Spirit. Therefore, we have power and my prayer is if our power has been distorted, let's transmit it in the right direction by empowering men not degrading them...

I build man up
I do not tear him down
I Am Woman

I encourage men
I don't discourage them
I Am Woman

I help him to achieve
Not bring him to his knees
I Am Woman

I speak words positively
Not words of negativity
I Am Woman

I am called to help him
I was not created to hinder them
I Am Woman

My mouth is used to uplift them
And my lips are used to embrace him
I Am Woman

Because my words have power
I speak words of empowerment
I Am Woman

Regardless of his situation
I have the power of elevation
I Am Woman

I am a lady of truth, gifted and name brand
Born to bring life into man's domain
I Am Woman

My inspiration for writing "***Super Mom***" was...

Sometimes I actually feel like this; able to see unseen things that are trying to affect my kids. Like God has enabled me to walk tall and see above incoming issues and circumstances. I am always sniffing and listening to what my kids are saying, who they are with, the way they say things and how they look when they say them...

I am Super Mom
Extraordinary, powerful and profound

A fierce warrior, a giant in command
Putting the laws down on demand

I fly like a bird covering my offspring
Protecting and guarding like superman

Praying and interceding on their behalf
For the angels to defend from the enemy's wrath

Monitoring and observing their every move
Feeding and implanting spiritual food

Listening for unusual sounds with bionic ears
Pulling down every negative thought out of the atmosphere

I'm a sign, an emblem a spiritual icon
Printed and embroidery as a symbol of time

A supernatural being a divine intervention
Armored to guard - I'm a super mom, did I mention?

An intrusion, interruption on the enemy's agenda
To protect and serve my children's interest

Super Mom

My inspiration for writing "***Imaginuity***" was...

I was asked by my brother-in-law, the musician to write a song on this topic. His explanation was that it's the gift of imagination & ingenuity that a woman has to maneuver and get what she wants; a gift that is good (if she uses it right) for man in which he is unaware of...

Imaginuity
A female's creativity
Resourceful, skillful, intuitive
To dream the impossibility
The execution of man's ability

Imaginuity
God's gift of ecstasy
Imagine you and me
In perfect harmony
Within her lies your peace

Imaginuity
Born of In-ti-ma-cy
He within she
In-to-me-see
What you and I can be

Imaginuity
Her discreet power of influence
Oblivious to him that she rules
Together we dominate and subdue
Imagine what I feel for you
Imaginuity – Imagine me in you

Imaginuity

My inspiration for writing "***Saint Barbara***" was...

I researched my name's meaning and it always said "stranger" or "foreigner". I didn't fully comprehend the terminology of these phrases until one day I was lead to St. Barbara where the name originated. And now I appreciate my name...

I was not happy with my first name
I thought it was common and somewhat bland
Until I stumbled on St. Barbara's pain
She redesigned the bathroom her father had planned

By ordering three windows to be put in it
Instead of the two her father had arranged originally
This she did because of her faith in the Holy Trinity
And when her father returned home he had a fit

Her wounds were burned and they beat her head
But Barbara found consolation in fasting and prayer
His plan for keeping his daughter in darkness had failed
Her love for God and the three lights had prevailed

He tried to kill her by the sword
But her prayers created an open wall
That miraculous translated her to a mountain gorge
Where flocks were watched by two shepherds

The history on the original Barbara
Were a saint, martyr and powerful intercessor
She was an extremely beautiful daughter
Of a wealthy heathen pagan father

Reading this story I have a different observation
On how I see my name because of her situation
I'm no longer a stranger or foreigner
I'm a beautiful, powerful child of God

Saint Barbara

The inspiration for writing "***An Attractive Contradiction***" was...

This poem was written because there was a friend that attempted to turn gay because of peer pressure and the only relief was to write it in poetry...

She's a beautiful girl with low self-esteem so she became a dike
The only reason why is because she wants to be liked
She got tricked by the demons so basically she's psych
She sags her pants and has a dark cloud so she never sees the light
But if she just turn right the light is so bright

They say she needs a father figure to make that big transfer
But no one listens to me because I say God is the answer
I remember all we use to talk about were boys back in the day
Now all she wears is multi colors because she says she gay
It hurt so bad I feel so betrayed

Now all her wonderful blessings will be delayed
I'm married to God so I hope she gets re-engaged
Everyday I pray she finds the right mate
Before her eyes close for good and it's too late
But right now all I can do is give God the praise

When she first told me I felt like she had died
Even til this day sometimes I still cry
I might not show it because it's only in the inside
But to tell you the truth my hearts eyes still isn't dried
I don't even like poetry but the way I feel I had to write

Mama said she'll change - well prove it
She the joker and everybody saw that movie - To me it's a dark night
I hope she gets her sight and come back to the light
I know I've been acting grouchy lately so excuse me
But it ain't spring time and things ain't looking too beautifully

I can't even go in public with her people think we on a date
So right now it's a very thin line between love and hate
She's killing me - her shots use to be 3-point range
She even made our basketball plans get rearranged
So all I have to say to you my friend is you need to change!

She don't want to look girly so she flatten the feminine part of her chest
Perpetrating her female attributes so others won't see that she has breast
My heart is still fragile it's in a healing process
I'm tired of competing with her lifestyle - this isn't no contest
But her gay ways try to shoot me - so I just have to wear a bulletproof vest...

An Attractive Contradiction

My inspiration for writing "***Barbara Jean Barbara Jean***" was…

I was asked by a musician to write a blues / rock song with a twist. So I wrote about a black cat. This poem needs no explanation, only imagination…

Barbara Jean
My fine black feline
Frisky valentine
Why you gotta be so mean
The way you crawl up me
You make me wanna scream
Barbara Jean
Barbara Jean

You're like a dose of morphine
Greek god of dreams
My putty cat that puts me to sleep
Make a dog wanna weep
Got me begging 'baby please'
Why you had to leave
Barbara Jean
Barbara Jean

My fine black feline
My sweet frisky valentine

Your furry kitty kat soothes my needs
Got all the dogs chasing you in the streets
Running after you – they can hardly breathe
Your sleek trim make'em weak in the knees
Make a dog wanna holler
Barbara Jean
Barbara Jean
Girl you know you're such a tease

My fine black feline
My sweet frisky valentine

Barbara Jean
Barbara Jean

My inspiration for writing "***Jesus Ministering Women's Liberty***" was...

I was asked to write a paper for a Women's Day Program and after completing the manuscript I turned it into poetry. So often in traditional churches women aren't allowed to minister or sit on the pulpit because of their gender. Some folks think that God doesn't speak or minister via women. Their depiction on women ministering can have others thinking that the Holy Spirit is prejudice. So I wrote this food for thought...

A Samaritan woman received living water at Jacob's well
When Jesus talked to her and broke the traditional curse from hell

A Canaanite woman had faith that was rare
She persistently begged Jesus and He answered her prayers

A poor widower gave a collection of two cents
And Jesus replied, "She gave more than the rich men"

A certain woman had an issue of blood for twelve years
Touched the hem of Jesus' garment and she was healed

A sinful woman washed with her tears, wiped with her hair, kissed and anointed Jesus' feet
He said to her, "Your sins are forgiven for you have showed much love to Me"

A woman caught in adultery was brought to Jesus for trickery
He said sin no more and saved her from a conspiracy

After His resurrection, Jesus first appeared to a woman asking, "Why weepest thou"
Revealed Himself to her and said, "Go and tell the disciples that I ascend to our God"

The Father sent an angel to visit a virgin lady
Favored and blessed are thee, into her planted His holy seed

From the poor to the sinful; out of Samaria; from Canaan; and into Galilee
Jesus has chosen, delivered, blessed and set women free

Jesus Ministering Women's Liberty

My inspiration for writing "***My Sistah***" was...

I was thinking that I've been deliberately, divinely attached to this girl on purpose and I accept it! I'm glad about it! I rejoice in it! And I love it...

She's sassy, she's classy
She's smart yet sometimes tart

She's funny –
She makes a lot of money

She's rarely wrong
She got it going on

She's faithful
Topped off with a scoop of graceful

She's strong-willed
She got madd skills

She's weird
She's fierce

She's swift
She's my gift

Wrapped in foreign silk
She's the one; she's my Sis

My Sistah

My inspiration for writing "***The "S" on My Chest***" was...

Every time my sister did something that appeared phenomenal and we asked her how she did that - she would always respond and say "I would show you this S on my chest – but I try not to show you all my super powers." So one day as she repeated this phrase to her husband for the fiftieth million times, he told her that you need to call Barbara and get her to write a poem about your super power phrase. And she did...

I would show u all my super powers
But I try not to show u the **"S"** on my chest
The strength under my vest
What's really inside my breast

U couldn't handle what u c
U probably would be terrified of me
Because my power is potency
And I walk in authority

I'll just hide it under my dress
Tucked away in secretness
Forcefully compelled and won't confess
A concealed weapon under duress

I won't show u all my super powers
I'll try not to show u
The **"S"** on my chest
The strength under my vest
What's really inside my breast

I'll keep it in secrecy
Secluded from the eyes to c
Obscured hidden from society
Confidentially armed in security
Discreetly covered in privacy
A powerful secret deep within me

The "S" on My Chest

My inspiration for writing "***Woman, Female, Eve – The First Lady***" was...

When I saw First Lady, Michelle Obama, walk the stage with her husband when it was announced that he had won presidency, I said to myself "Look at my lips and look at my hips on that stage." She represented every woman of color on the planet and I was proud. I was proud that the African-American female figure was on display and never again will it be put to shame, considered too thick, looked at to be too dark, too full or too much....

Look at my legs, my hips, and my thighs
The method in my walk, the talk in my stride
The confidence and smile in my dark brown eyes

The way I walk with poise and swing my hips
The smile that embraces you with thick full lips
The soft warm touch of my mouth in a kiss

My elongated neck and black coarse hair
My curvaceous figure fashioned like a pear
That persuades your eyes to look and stare

The round plump shape of my behind
That's attached to my arched waistline
Entwines a rhythmic tune in your mind

The voluptuous formation of my breast
That holds the softness of my chest
And embraces you with gentleness

I Am who I am - chosen to be
Tender, soft, gentle and sweet
Woman, Female, Eve

– I am The First Lady

Woman, Female, Eve – The First Lady

V
Book Of Brothers

My inspiration for writing "***A Letter to My Father***" was ...

I was thinking that God truly is my father and we have a personal relationship. As I meditated on that thought I was inspired to communicate with Him personally as well as reverence his sovereignty.

I was reminded that Enoch walked with God (Gen. 5: 24); therefore Enoch had a personal relationship with God. Abraham was a friend of God (James 2: 23); therefore Abraham had a personal relationship with God. And last but certainly not least Jesus appears on the scene and introduces us to a personal side of God we had never known, Our Father...

Dear Father,

I was thinking of You and decided to drop You a few lines;
And let You know what's on my mind.

The things You do that I love so much about You;
Like loving me regardless of what I did or didn't do.

You have pulled me out of so many jams.
Your Word has given me wisdom to understand who I am.

There are times when You make me feel like I'm Your favorite;
When You whisper in my ear and tell me one of Your secrets.

Father, I love being alone with You when no one else is around;
When silence partners with us and there's no need for sound.

I love just calling You, hearing You, needing no reason or explanation
To vent and You listen, allowing me to find solutions to my frustrations.

Father, thank You for always being there for me;
For never leaving nor forsaking me,

For sacrificing and caring unselfishly,
For Your providence in supplying all my needs,

For Your preeminence in always going before me,
For Your sovereignty in hovering over me,

For covering and sheltering me,
For protecting and shielding me.

If I have never said how much You mean to me;
You surely are the greatest Father this world has ever seen

A Letter to My Father

My inspiration for writing "***My Brother***" was...

I wanted to write a positive poem about brothers and the first thought that came to my mind was my love for my brother. This poem's depiction is exact to its words...

I have a brother like no other
He answers when I call and is there for me
He doesn't let me fall he takes care of me

I have a brother like no other
He fills in the gap where there is lack
He gets me out of traps and picks up the slack

I have a brother like no other
He always comes when I need him
He love the kids every last one of them

I have a brother like no other
He's so crazy - he's a lot of fun
He's so amazing - he's a special son

I have a brother like no other
He is very unusual and extraordinary to me
He's not superficial you better believe

I have a brother like no other
He work on cars a certified mechanic
I think he's from mars and he's a maniac

I have a brother like no other
He tickles me in the side all the time
And knows I don't like it - he messes with my mind

I have a brother like no other
He drives really fast - you will be taken for a ride
Hold on to your ass - because you think you might die

I have a brother like no other
He's kind hearted and takes good care of my mother
I'm glad he's my brother - I wouldn't trade him for another

My Brother

My inspiration for writing "***Am I My Brother's Keeper?***" was...

I was asked to write a paper for a Men's Day Program and after completing the manuscript I turned it into poetry. This poem is food for thought...

I have a question. Am I my brother's keeper?

If I know my brother has gone astray and can't find his way

Am I my brother's keeper?

If I know my brother is homeless and has nowhere to stay

Am I my brother's keeper?

If I know my brother is hungry and don't have a piece of bread

Am I my brother's keeper?

If I know my brother is burden and don't have the strength to pray

Am I my brother's keeper?

If I know my brother has backslide and gone back to his old ways

Am I my brother's keeper?

If I know my brother was thirsty and was about to dehydrate

Am I my brother's keeper?

If I know my brother has trespassed should I forgive him everyday

Am I my brother's keeper?

Am I My Brother's Keeper?

My inspiration for writing "***Fatherless 2007***" was...

Every year during the second week in June, Father's Day is celebrated. This specific year I got sick of hearing and seeing it in every store. It was advertised everywhere and I felt like it was being stuffed down my throat. So in order to get the stuffing out this is what I wrote...

Father – what does that mean to me
Daddy – is that a real human being
Pops in my world is a rare species
My old man gave up his paternity

Since my childhood he has been extinct
And because of that we were never in sync
No point of reference –there was no link
My senses cannot identify a father's instinct

The title, the term is foreign to me
The feel, the knowledge of being in his arms safely
The sniff, the smell of a father's security
Has anyone seen him – his nickname is daddy

Why do they celebrate this day?
Like it's a national holiday
Does he know I have a birthday?
What do they mean by Father's Day?

I'm so sick of not knowing
So I regurgitated this poem
When I woke up this morning
But I'm still sleeping on this term

Don't take these words personally
This thing is strange and grotesque to me
Abandonment is my reality
Because fatherless is what I see

Fatherless 2007

My inspiration for writing *"**A New Father**"* was...

This poem was written as a reminder of the missing presence of my biological father. It continually reminds me of the truth; that I really have a Father...

I've got a new Father – not quite new
He's been Our Father since creation

I have accepted the ultimate invitation
Deliverance from the power of sin - the call of salvation

Renewing my mind through prayer and studying for transformation
I have been reinstated through the power of reconciliation

The Father and Son resides in me - A holy habitation
His Holy Spirit gives me comfort and confirmation

He communicates with me through revelation
And because of Christ I no longer live in condemnation

I have been saved by grace and separated for His sanctification
And washed in His blood for purification

Jesus dying on the cross is my justification
I now reign with Christ in heavenly places

I will forever serve God a lifetime of dedication
Devoted for God's use set apart for consecration

Brought back to God through restoration
Magnifying and praising His Name in glorification

A New Father

VI
Book
Of
Serenity
&
Thoughts

My inspiration for writing "***A Quiet Place***" was...

A quiet place located inside of me is where I write from and this poem portrays that...

I'm in a space of limitless
In a place called timeless

Where I can free style
For a little or a long while

And meditate on what I want to say
Lettering the words in my own way

Lost in my world internally
From the cares of life externally

Stirring up the gift inside of me
Penciling on paper for others to see

This is where I write from
Amongst the stars underneath the sun

Within a place where I can hide
In a moment in space right outside of time

A Quiet Place

My inspiration for writing "***Expressions of Me – Reflections of the Day***" was...

I was sitting outside enjoying the outdoors when these thoughts ran through my mind. So I decided to put them in words...

Sweet, smooth, melody
Picking up the pieces of my dream

Flying, floating, riding high
Wings of eagles touching the sky

Alone, me, myself and I
An inward peaceful lullaby

Cultivating, captivating, relaxation
The results of my adoration

Imagining, meditating, drifting to sleep
Is the mood I'm in – this is liberty

Perfect moments – good times
Are the thoughts cruising thru my mind

You ask me – what do I say
Expressions of me – Reflections of the day

Expressions of Me - Reflections of the Day

My inspiration for writing "***A Secret Place***" was...

There are times when you just want to get away from everyday cares of life and become hidden and get refreshed - a secret place; like going to a retreat without having to physically travel. But you can spiritually travel to a place within you; a place where God resides - His spirit within you. A secret place...

A secret place
Where I feel safe

A secret place
Where I can rest and lay

A secret place
Where I can escape

A secret place
From the cares of the day

A secret place
Where I can fly far away

A secret place
Where I can surrender and pray

A secret place
Sorting the things in my head

A secret place
Where I long to stay

A secret place
Where I can see my Father's face

A Secret Place

My inspiration for writing "***Filtering Thoughts***" was...

I had felt rejected by a friend and was bitter even though the cause was my own senseless actions. And because of this when I looked at him his appearance literally changed; whereas I use to see him as beautiful – he no longer looked the same. As I searched myself and considered my actions I discovered that I needed correction and my thoughts were being filtered due to inner bitterness...

Are your eyes deceived
Are you able to interpret what you have received

Has it been diluted through a filtering system
A false conception of deceptive listening

Really – what do you hear
Entering into your ear

Your mamma, your daddy; your history
A drama, comedy or a mystery

Can you figure it out without a doubt
Does it need to be repeated – or even shouted

The entry is clouded, the canal is blocked
There's no access, the pathway is stopped

And being infiltrated through an alternate route
In danger or being wiped out – as planted seed unable to sprout

Cannot be retrieved; the data is lost
Through shadowed, hidden, obscured thoughts

Filtering Thoughts

My inspiration for writing “***Distractions***” was…

I wanted a deeper relationship with God and knew that this will take more intimate time. Something was invading my space between me trying to see my Savior’s face and pulling me from my God’s grace. It has a name and it is called **Distractions**…

Distractions come to get you off track
So others won't follow the print of your impact
To cause your train of thought to be hijacked
And steal your ideal in a sudden attack

To bring your destiny to a cease
That your dreams won't be released
And you will continue to fall asleep
So that your mission won't be complete

Why do you think He gives you dreams
This is not just a fantasy
A message from God to you and me
To bring to pass the impossibility

For Him to enable your inability
And bring His kingdom into reality
To show forth His image and creativity
So that others may wake up and see

The mighty hand of His authority
A witness walking in integrity
Displaying His splendor and majesty
A vessel of honor carrying His glory

Distractions

My inspiration for writing "***The Wisdom and Victory in a Game***" was...

As I watched my daughter play basketball over the years, I notice these observations...

The team who is the hungriest shall eat the victory

Never take your opponent for granted

A good coach can take a weak team and triumph over defeat

A team is a unit as one regardless of the format of the circle

Once a team believes they are one, they will know each others' game

When a team becomes one every game will be won

One should always glorify God in the gift of the game

A coach's weight can muzzle the gift in a player and suppress it from emerging

You must eat basketball, sleep basketball and bleed basketball to be the champ in basketball

Become one with the game and you will taste victory

You should love the game - not be in love with the game

Games are played to have fun not as burden and laboring in an activity

A few mistakes are an opponent's wish list

The victory is not given to the most powerful nor to the quickest but to the one that continues to the end

My inspiration for writing "***Deep Within" was***...

An artist asked me to write a poem from a picture he had drawn...

Like deep within the sea

Is water without measure

Lies deep within me

Hidden talent and treasure

So I will search to see

The depths of Heaven and Eternity

The journey I am to take expeditiously

What is it I have been called to be...

Deep Within

My inspiration for writing "***Pane of Pain***" was...

I was helping a friend sort through some troublous times and in doing so, I happen to reveal some things about me that I wanted to stay hidden. I wasn't ready to face the past because for me to re-visit it was to relive it; and that took a lot of energy...

God trusted and allowed me to see my friend's pain

But when the light was shone on me, I ran

I didn't want him to think I was insane

And allow him to see through my windowpane

Distressing emotions of tears flowing like rain

From the striking terror of a mother's hand

An abandoned infantile that a father had disdain

A scorned child so full of shame

Wandering and wondering who's to blame

Pane of Pain

My inspiration for writing "***They Can't Do It Without Me***" was...

As I was pondering on the greatness I know my kids will grow to be, a still small voice spoke inside of me and said "They can't do it without you; they can only go so far alone." So I wrote this poem...

They can't do it without me
Obtain their highest degree
To become a celebrity
To be all they can be
It's bigger than their eyes can see
More than they can ever believe
Without me - there's no dream

I'm speaking of a reality
Speaking from my history
The truth about a mystery
Sharing with you the lesson for today
The seed will not grow if not cultivated
The arrow will not go far this way
So attend your ears and hear what I say

Children need their parents to stay
In their lives constantly
So that they won't become prey
To the systems of this world today
Not having to fight and pray
The ghosts of their yesterday
All because their parents decided not to stray

They Can't Do It Without Me

My inspiration for writing "***A Yearning Deep Within***" was...

There's a constant yearning for greatness to be birth from within and it tries to come out, it cries to come out. I believe that this yearning is within everyone.
A Pulitzer Prize will be awarded due to this poem...

There's a yearning deep within
That ceases to come to an end
Until its dawning start to begin

In anticipation of its fruition
Starving from the pain of mal-nutrition
Forever waiting for its petition

Like a stronghold or an addiction
Patiently awaiting its rendition
For you to discover its definition

The time of its illumination
To show forth its dedication
Bringing you into destination

That it may face creation
In unison with celebration
Receiving its standing ovation

Taking you high into elevation
Bursting with joy in appreciation
Dispersing fame with gratification

Receiving its satisfaction
That it obtained your reaction
And now you are the main attraction

A Yearning Deep Within

VII
Book
Of
Tributes

My inspiration for writing "***Stephenson Girls Varsity 09***" was...

I was asked by the President of the Tip-off Club to recite a poem for the 2009 Banquet, which inspired me to write this poem. The statements in this piece are factual....

Allow me to introduce Stephenson Girl's Varsity '09'
The Jaguar Defenders – Powerful Felines

Let us begin with the starting five
Hydaaiyah known for the jump shot at the free-throw line

Pass it to Kayla our 3-point shooter - she'll make it every time
We then have Shareka that'll steal the ball on the sly

In come Erika that girl know how to draw those fouls
Let's not forget Nikki – she'll take it to the hoop with a drive

That's Stephenson starters for '09'
When we need defense Coach will call on Ty

She'll cross them over with a pass so fly
Straight to Jazz with a lay-up on her right side

#21, Dannie, knows how to get the rebound
She'll go up strong and knock her opponent to the ground

When we need some 3's its Marissa's time
To catch n shoot and turn the game around

To take it to the hole we'll call on 'O'
She'll dribble straight down to the defenders court

Then come Bria – put her in the right spot
She'll turn and shoot a quick hot shot

In come Santia to put pressure on the ball
She'll stop her opponent like a spy ware firewall

That's the Stephenson Girl's Varsity '09'
The Jaguar Defenders– Powerful Felines

The cat that attacks with a quick pounce
The beast that kills its prey with a single bound

Stephenson Girls Varsity '09

My inspiration for writing "***A Tribute to My Aunt***" was...

This poem was written in memory of my past Aunt. She was a very spiritual lady who desired that her kids were saved and knew God...

For me to live is Christ and to die is gain
I have no more worries and no more pain

I am free from this world's stress and heartaches
I've gone up yonder where He has prepared my place

Let not your heart be troubled; believe in God, believe also in Christ
Because it is through Him that I've passed into eternal life

He has come and received me to Himself; for where He is I am also
My desire is that you too go, to the place you know, the way you know

For Jesus is the way, the truth and the life
No one comes to the Father except through Christ

For I was weary and He gave me peace
I was burden and he gave me relief

I was tired and He gave me rest
I am healed and free from sickness

So come all that labor and are heavy laden to Christ
For His yoke is easy and His burden is light

For Christ I have lived, in Christ I have died and with Christ I now lay
I have fought the good fight, I have finished the race and I have kept the faith

A Tribute to My Aunt

My inspiration for writing "***Can You See God's Hand?***" was...

I was asked to write a poem in memory of a grandmother that lived 100+ years – Her family's term of endearment was "Mymee"...

I greet in you in the Name of Our Lord and Savior Jesus Christ.

The Name that woke you up this morning;

The Name that started you on your way;

The Name that is above every name;

The Name in which I ask this question; can you see God's hand?

Are you a part of the Master's plan?

Or do you just exist in His promise land?

You are called for a purpose, do you understand?

Oh yes, I AM have arrived; the God of a second chance;

A third, fourth and another until Christ returns again.

The God who grace a mother to live over a hundred years to enjoy life, longevity, family and friends.

The God that continues to knock on the door of your heart and ask, "Can I come in?"

The God, who wrapped Himself in a baby, grew as our Savior and dwelt among man.

That died on the cross that you and I may have fellowship with Him again.

That can give you peace in times of grief that surpasses all understanding.

That reminds you over and over again, "You don't have to live that way son of man."

The God who said, "Whosoever will let him come"; and answer the question, will you give God your hand?

Can You See God's Hand?

My inspiration for writing “***He Never Left Me***” was...

I was a mother who had a baby at a very young age. The baby passed and the only way I can feel better is to write. This poem was written in memory of my baby that passed at 4 month...

Losing someone is terrible
Being jilted is horrible

I was jilted in the month of November
A month I'll always remember

He was born on July the tenth
He was so beautiful and content

When he came into this world he was new
I kept saying to myself, "He's too good to be true"

He was alert of everything around
He always made me happy, he never let me down

He was an angel I must say
As far as I'm concern, he never left me; he never went away

He Never Left Me

My inspiration for writing "***The Journey***" was...

My best friend's son was getting married and she wanted to leave words of wisdom with him. So she asked me to write a poem for his rehearsal dinner and this is what manifested...

The Journey from there to where we are
Was a distance reserved more near than far
A time of travel that stayed in my heart
A movement from one place to another we have chartered
Was the past waiting on the future into the present - that will not recur?
Is where we are – in the now – where I will start.

A new beginning; a new chapter in your life
With a new book, a new look, a new wife
But **The Journey** had not always been nice
The Journey took a lot of patience and sacrifice
Your dad had to cover many miles at night
Of highways and by-ways for you to have a good life

We might have made mistakes along the way
In spite of it all you turned out okay
With faith in God on my knees I always pray
That my children will never from God stray away
And that He will give them everyday
Daily bread from His storehouse for them to accumulate

In fact you have done better than okay
Because most sons have no mentors today
But God has blessed you with two dads in your days
I am proud of the sons in which God has gave
The fruit of my womb – the joy in my old age
My male child – the one I call Chase

Our goal was to give you a place called home
So take heed to the following psalms -
Keep in your heart that family is number one
And always know you're by no means alone
Never take for granted the kindness of anyone
Remember we're here today and tomorrow gone
So make wise your decisions my special son
The Journey

About the Author

BJ Whittington currently resides in the Atlanta, Ga. metropolitan area. She is a native of Donaldsonville, La. and has been writing poetry since high school. She is also co-author of *Mama Down The Bayou Recipes with Shopping List*, a Southern Creole cookbook with shopping lists and event timelines. She is currently working on her next literary composition.

www.ingramcontent.com/pod-product-compliance
Ingram Content Group UK Ltd.
Pitfield, Milton Keynes, MK11 3LW, UK
UKHW021052270726
13967UKWH00012B/633